Congressional
Research
Service

Distributional Effects of Taxes on Corporate Profits, Investment Income, and Estates

Jane G. Gravelle
Senior Specialist in Economic Policy

Sean Lowry
Analyst in Public Finance

December 27, 2012

Congressional Research Service

7-5700

www.crs.gov

RL32517

CRS Report for Congress
Prepared for Members and Committees of Congress

Summary

Tax reductions enacted in 2001-2004 reduce the effective tax rate on capital income in several different ways. Taxes on capital arise from individual taxes on dividends, interest, capital gains, and income from non-corporate businesses (proprietorships and partnerships). Reductions in marginal tax rates, as well as some tax benefits for business, reduce these taxes. Taxes on capital income also arise from corporate profits taxes, which are affected not only by rate reductions but also by changes to provisions affecting depreciation, interest deductions, other deductions and credits. Finally, taxes can be imposed on capital income through the estate and gift tax.

Tax cuts on capital income through capital gains rate reductions, estate and gift tax reductions, and dividend relief are estimated to cost about $57 billion per year, with about half that amount attributable to the estate and gift tax. Lower ordinary tax rates also affect income from unincorporated businesses. These tax cuts are temporary and proposals to make some or all of them permanent are expected. Bonus depreciation appears less likely to be extended.

While there are many factors used to evaluate the effects of these tax revisions, one of them is the distributional effect. This report addresses those distributional issues, in the context of behavioral responses.

Data suggest that taxes on capital income tend to fall more heavily on high-income individuals. All types of capital income are concentrated in higher-income classes. For example, the top 2.8% of tax returns (with adjusted gross income over $200,000 in 2009) have 26% of income, 19% of wages, 39% of interest, 39% of dividends, and 57% of capital gains. Taking into account a very broad range of capital assets, a 2012 Treasury study found that the top 1% of the population has about 19% of total income and about 12% of labor income, but receives almost half of total capital income. Estate and gift taxes are especially concentrated in the higher incomes: prior to the tax cuts enacted in 2001-2004, only 2% of estates paid the estate tax at all.

If there is a significant reduction in savings in response to capital income taxes, in the long run the tax could be shifted to labor and thus become a regressive tax. Some growth models are consistent with such a view, but generally theory suggests that increases in taxes on capital income could either decrease or increase savings, depending on a variety of model assumptions and particularly depending on the disposition of the revenues. There are also many reasons to be skeptical of these models, which presume a great deal of skill and sophistication on the part of individuals. New models of bounded rationality suggest that taxes on capital income are likely to have no effect or decrease saving, as individuals rely on common rules of thumb such as saving a fixed fraction of income and saving for a target.

Empirical evidence in general does not suggest significant savings responses, as savings rates and pre-tax returns to capital have been relatively constant over long periods of time despite significant changes in tax rate. If capital income taxes do not reduce saving, these taxes fall on capital income and add to the progressivity of the income tax system. This report does not track legislation and will not be updated.

Contents

Tables

Appendixes

Contacts

Introduction

Tax reductions enacted in 2001 through 2004, as well as some under consideration, reduce the effective tax rate on capital income in several different ways. Taxes on capital arise from individual taxes on dividends, interest, capital gains, and income from non-corporate businesses (proprietorships and partnerships). Reductions in marginal tax rates as well as some tax benefits for business reduce these taxes. Taxes on capital income also arise from corporate profits taxes, which are affected not only by rate reductions but also by changes to provisions affecting depreciation, interest deductions, other deductions, and credits. Finally, taxes can be imposed on capital income through the estate and gift tax.

Some of these provisions were originally to expire in 2010 or earlier but were extended for an additional two years. Further extensions are under consideration. Bonus depreciation was deliberately set to be temporary, and expired in 2004. It was reinstated in 2008 and extended on several occasions as a stimulus during the recent recession, but is not included in any current legislation. The largest of the reductions, measured by estimated revenue cost, is a one-year extension of the marginal individual rate reductions, which is estimated to cost approximately $94 billion.[1] Other revenue losses include the estate and gift tax repeal at a cost $31 billion, and the reduction in tax rates on dividends and capital gains at a cost of approximately $26 billion.[2] In addition to extensions of various tax reductions, income tax reform, including reform of corporate and business taxes, may be considered, which could also affect capital income tax burdens.

Although many issues surround these tax changes, one of them is the extent to which they benefit higher- or lower-income individuals. The eventual consequences of these tax provisions depend on the behavioral responses to tax cuts, which also drive issues of incentive effects and economic growth. This report addresses these distributional issues, in the context of behavioral responses.

The first section of this paper provides general data on the distribution of capital income of various types, as a background to discussing the incidence issues. The next section discusses how behavioral responses could alter the distributional effects, examining both shifts in the types of assets held and changes in savings rates.

Data on the Distribution of Income by Type and Class

Capital income may be earned directly by individuals in operating their own businesses or as passive income from lending or investing in corporate stocks. Income from unincorporated businesses is not separated into labor and capital income, but the distribution of income of different types can be compared by examining passive capital income sources. There are three major types of passive capital income: interest on debt, dividends on corporate stock, and capital

---

[1] U.S. Congress, Joint Committee on Taxation, JCS-64-12, "Estimated Revenue Effects Of H.R. 8, The 'Job Protection And Recession Prevention Act Of 2012,'" July 24, 2012, at https://www.jct.gov/publications.html?func=startdown& id=4476.

[2] Ibid.

gains (which arise from the sale of stock and from the sale of other assets). **Table 1** provides data on the distribution of this income.

Table 1. Share of Income by Source by Adjusted Gross Income Class (AGI), 2009

Income Class ($000s)	Share of Returns (%)	Share of AGI (%)	Share of Wages (%)	Share of Interest (%)[a]	Share of Dividends (%)	Share of Capital Gains (%)[b]	Share of Tax-exempt Interest
<0	1.8	-2.6	0.4	5.6	2.6	4.3	4.5
0-15	25.0	3.6	3.5	5.5	2.7	-1.0	2.6
15-30	21.4	8.7	9.1	7.1	3.4	-0.3	4.0
30-50	17.9	12.9	14.0	8.4	4.8	-0.1	5.8
50-75	13.3	15.1	15.9	10.4	7.1	1.2	8.8
75-100	8.2	13.0	13.7	8.0	6.5	1.9	7.5
100-200	9.6	23.6	24.9	16.4	16.2	7.5	17.4
200-500	2.3	11.9	11.1	11.9	15.5	11.7	17.8
>500	0.2	9.5	4.2	26.8	33.2	64.9	21.9

Source: CRS analysis of Internal Revenue Service Statistics of Income data, All Returns: Sources of Income, Adjustments, and Tax Items (Table 1.4), 2009, at http://www.irs.gov/file_source/pub/irs-soi/09in14ar.xls.

a. Interest is defined as taxable interest plus ordinary dividends, less qualified dividends.

b. Capital gains are defined as taxable net gain minus net short-term capital gain. This column reports gain on sales of capital assets, and does not include capital gains distributions on mutual funds.

Table 1 demonstrates several aspects of the distribution of capital income. First, as in the case of all income, the distribution is very uneven, with larger shares accruing to very small portions of the population. For example, the under $30,000 adjusted gross income class has 48% of the returns but only 10% of income, 13% of wages, 18% of taxable interest income, 9% of taxable dividends and 3% of taxable capital gains. Those over $200,000 had 26% of income, 19% of wages, 39% of taxable interest income, 39% of taxable dividends, and 57% of taxable capital gains.

Secondly, on the whole capital income is more concentrated among higher-income individuals than is wage income and the concentration varies by type. Capital gains are more heavily concentrated among higher-income individuals than is income from dividends, and dividends are more concentrated than interest. Higher-income individuals are more likely to be risk takers and invest in stocks and bonds so that both dividends and capital gains are more concentrated in higher-income classes than is interest income. The greater concentration of capital gains as compared to dividends may be partly due to the preference of higher-income individuals for growth stocks, partly due to the fact that a lot of interest is effectively reported as dividends because it is funneled through mutual funds, and partly due to the fact that sales of capital assets also reflects sales of real property (also concentrated in high-income classes). High-income individuals would also tend to prefer investments that would have otherwise been subject to higher individual tax rates, and so may be more concentrated in capital gains and stocks for that reason. (Although corporate source income is taxed more heavily than non-corporate income, this rate is essentially a flat rate and there is no tax benefit to higher-income individuals. At the personal tax level, however, high-income individuals benefit from the lower capital gains rates more than lower- and middle-income individuals, because of the higher spread between the ordinary and capital gains tax rate.)

Note that there are also significant amounts of capital income that are not subject to tax. One such source of income, tax exempt municipal bonds, is reported in **Table 1**. There are much larger amounts of interest held in pensions and IRAs; in fact about half of interest and dividends are not taxable for this reason. The implicit rent from owning consumer durables, most importantly owner occupied housing, is not subject to tax.

If individuals did not change their behavior in response to a tax change, then the effect of tax cuts or increases for these types of income could be measured by applying the change in the tax rates to income. Cuts in capital gains tax would most favor higher-income individuals, but in general, all tax cuts on capital income are likely to benefit higher-income individuals.

Table 1 does not contain any information about the estate and gift tax. However, the estate tax is highly concentrated among top asset classes, with only 2.1% of decedents paying estate taxes in 2000 (before the recent round of tax cuts).

Table 1 also does not contain direct information about corporate source income, but since that income is ultimately received as dividends and capital gains, the data also suggest that corporate taxes, were there to be no behavioral response, would fall on higher-income individuals.

Based on this distributional data, capital income taxes fall on higher-income individuals and contribute to the progressivity of the tax system.

Shifting and Incidence of Taxes: Effects Arising from Portfolio Shifts

This analysis, however, is incomplete for two reasons: portfolio shifts and possible effects on savings behavior. Portfolio shifts are considered first.

Holding aggregate assets as fixed, there is no behavioral response unless returns on different types of assets are taxed differently. In general, more assets will be allocated to those activities or forms of investment whose returns are favored by the tax system.

In a classic economics article that focused on the response to a differential tax—in this case the corporate income tax—the analysis showed that the likely outcome of such behavioral response is that the burden of the tax falls on all owners of capital.[3] This behavioral response arose from the migration of capital out of the more heavily taxed sector as the post-tax return falls, and into the more lightly taxed sector. As capital migrates, the sector with the reduced capital stock will experience a higher pre-tax return (because capital is relatively scarce compared to the other

---

[3] See Arnold C. Harberger, "The Incidence of the Corporate Income Tax," *Journal of Political Economy*, vol. 79, June 1962, pp. 215-240. This outcome has persisted through many different ways of modeling the coexistence of a corporate and noncorporate sector. Although these different approaches have found different efficiency effects they all tend to point to the burden falling largely on capital and either slightly harming or slightly benefitting labor income. For a brief overview see Jane G. Gravelle, *The Economic Effects of Taxing Capital Income* (Cambridge: MIT Press, 1994), pp. 79-82.

sectors), while the sectors with the increased capital stock will experience a lower pre-tax return. This process occurs until after-tax returns (adjusted for risk) are once again equated. Capital owners in the tax-favored sector bear part of the burden through lower pre-tax returns and capital owners in the taxed sector have some of the original burden reduced through higher pre-tax returns. This shifting effect can, however, only occur for the "normal" return to capital (the return earned by competitive firms); excess returns due, for example, to market power should be capitalized in the value of the firm: an increase in tax produces a one-time fall in value that falls on the current owners.

Labor could benefit slightly or share some small part of the burden, but in general to examine the burden of, say the corporate tax, one would want to attribute the tax to owners of capital in general. Thus to determine the distribution across income classes it is necessary to determine the distribution of capital and labor income.

A Treasury study estimates the distribution of capital, labor, and all income by population quintile (with some finer divisions at the top), as reported in **Table 2**. This analysis confirms the earlier findings that suggest capital income is especially concentrated at high levels. The top 1% has more than 30% of capital income but only 10% of labor income.

Table 2. Distribution of Income: Capital, Labor, and Total

Family Income Quintile[a]	Percentage of Capital Income	Percentage of Labor Income	Percentage of Total Income
Lowest[b]	0.8	1.9	2.3
Second	2.3	6.8	6.8
Third	5.2	12.4	11.8
Fourth	9.7	21.8	19.7
Highest	80.9	56.8	59.9
Top 10%	72.8	39.1	44.5
Top 5%	65.6	26.8	33.4
Top 1%	49.8	11.5	18.6

Source: Julie-Anne Cronin, Emily Y. Lin, Laura Power, and Michael Cooper, *Distributing the Corporate Income Tax: Revised U.S. Treasury Methodology*, Office of Tax Analysis Technical Paper 5, May 2012, p. 24, at http://www.treasury.gov/resource-center/tax-policy/tax-analysis/Documents/OTA-T2012-05-Distributing-the-Corporate-Income-Tax-Methodology-May-2012.pdf.

a. Quintiles begin at cash income of Second $18,094; Third $34,910; Fourth $57,714; Highest $99,912; Top 10% $145,011; Top 5% $205,697; and Top 1% $499,329 (at 2012 income levels).

b. Families with negative incomes are excluded from the lowest income quintile.

Thus while portfolio shifts should be taken into account in determining the burden of capital income taxes, since overall capital is concentrated towards higher-income individuals, a tax on capital income is likely to fall on higher-income individuals, even considering shifts in the allocation of capital. Hence, capital income taxes contribute to the progressivity of the tax system, even if they are applied at a flat rate (as is essentially the case of the corporate tax).

There is one potential reservation to this argument, even in the context of a fixed savings rate, namely the effect of capital income taxation in an open economy. When capital is migrating across sectors, labor is also free to migrate as well as wages and prices change. When capital migrates abroad, however, labor does not have the same freedom. Thus it is possible that the burden of capital income tax shifts to labor for this reason.

Indeed, in a very specific set of circumstances one can find that the entire burden of a tax imposed in one country is shifted to labor and since the share of labor income received by higher-income individuals is less than the share of total income, then capital income taxes would be regressive rather than progressive.

The circumstances for this outcome, however, are very narrow: the tax must be applied on a territorial basis (that is, only applied to capital used in the country, not capital owned by the country's citizens), capital investments must be perfectly substitutable across different countries, the country must be a small country, products must be perfect substitutes, and there are no returns from market power. Moreover, there must be no response to a change in tax rates from the trading partners. These conditions do not apply to the United States, which is a large country where personal level taxes are applied on a residence basis and even corporate taxes are not entirely territorial. Moreover imperfect substitutability of assets or of products can cause less and even none of the tax to fall on labor, even in the absence of market power, and the empirical evidence suggests that such is the case. Finally, with inflation, debt financed capital can actually experience a subsidy at the firm level (because nominal interest payments are deductible) and if debt is more substitutable than equity (which is likely) an increase in the corporate tax could actually cause a capital inflow rather than a capital outflow. [4]

Thus, introducing an open economy is not likely to change the conclusion that the ultimate burden of capital income taxes falls on capital in general and therefore falls more heavily on higher-income individuals, even in the limited case of the corporate tax.

---

[4] For a more detailed discussion of corporate tax incidence, see CRS Report RL34229, *Corporate Tax Reform: Issues for Congress*, by Jane G. Gravelle and Thomas L. Hungerford. In the past, the Congressional Budget Office, the Treasury Department, and the Urban-Brookings Tax Policy Center attributed 100% of the tax to capital income. Recently all three organizations have moved to assigning a small share to labor income. The Congressional Budget Office assigns 25%, the Treasury Department 18%, and the Urban-Brookings Tax Policy Center 20%. The Department of Treasury and the Tax Policy center assign a large share of the tax to stockholders based on the idea that a large share of income is supra-normal returns. This share is based in part on an estimate of the share of the corporate tax that is above a risk-free return. While some part of this return may be rent, it probably also largely reflects risk premiums. There is, however, little justification for assigning the part of a return due to anticipated risk as an "excess return" since such returns compensate for risk-taking. With risk and imperfect loss offset, the tax on the risk premium falls in part in the same way as the normal return, in part on taxpayers to the extent the tax reduces the variance of return but increases variance in revenues, and to some extent disappears because the government is less risk-adverse than individuals. The Congressional Budget Office allocates the tax based on results from general equilibrium models, modified for certain issues such as debt finance and rents. For further explanation, see Congressional Budget Office, *The Distribution of Household Income and Federal Taxes, 2008 and 2009*, at http://cbo.gov/sites/default/files/cbofiles/attachments/43373-06-11-HouseholdIncomeandFedTaxes.pdf; Julie-Anne Cronin, Emily Y. Lin, Laura Power, and Michael Cooper, *Distributing the Corporate Income Tax: Revised U.S. Treasury Methodology*, Office of Tax Analysis Technical Paper 5, May 2012, at http://www.treasury.gov/resource-center/tax-policy/tax-analysis/Documents/OTA-T2012-05-Distributing-the-Corporate-Income-Tax-Methodology-May-2012.pdf; Jim Nunns, *How the TPC Distributes the Corporate Income Tax*, Urban-Brookings Tax Policy Center, at http://www.taxpolicycenter.org/UploadedPDF/412651-Tax-Model-Corporate-Tax-Incidence.pdf.

The Effect of the Savings Response

The burden of a capital income tax could be shifted, in all or in part, to labor, if individuals respond to the reduction in return by reducing savings.[5] However, such an effect is not at all certain. On a theoretical basis, in a model of optimizing individuals, an increase in the rate of return can lead to more savings or less savings depending on income and substitution effects (that is, lower incomes cause one to consume less in every time period, while substitution effects cause consumption to shift over time). The outcome depends on a number of important issues and model assumptions. Secondly, the presumption that individuals can make the complex optimizing decisions about saving that are depicted in these models is questionable. Indeed, there is considerable reason to believe that individuals may employ rule-of-thumb guidelines to saving behavior that suggest that taxes on capital either have no effect or increase savings. This view is bolstered by empirical evidence that suggests savings rates tend to be relatively steady over time rather than engaging in the dramatic swings that are predicted by certain optimizing models.

To interpret the empirical evidence, it must be related to a particular theory, so the first subsection lays out alternative models and approaches and their theoretical implications: the Ramsey model, the life-cycle model, and a discussion of bounded rationality. The following subsection reviews briefly some of the empirical evidence.

Theoretical Background: Models of Saving

The earliest model of economic growth, called the Solow model, simply took the savings rate to be fixed. Like much of the macroeconomic theory developed before the 1970s, the model was developed to explain empirical observations. Models of economic cycles were needed to explain depressions and recessions, and models of growth needed to reflect the stylized facts of steady growth of output and productivity in the U.S. postwar period. The Solow model with its fixed savings rate was consistent with both a steady state growth in output per capita in the U.S. economy, as well as a savings rate that seemed to show no trend.

Economists were dissatisfied with those models, which were not built up from individual optimizing decisions as are other models in economics, and many new macroeconomic model variations developed. As a result, students in modern macroeconomics study many types of models. In the area of economic growth, these new models were intertemporal models which allowed individuals to choose consumption over time—that is to make savings decisions that responded to the prices and quantities in the economy. Many of these models continued to treat technological advance as exogenous and characterized by steady state growth.[6] Of these models,

---

[5] Two issues of the Economic Report of the President during the decade that the tax cuts were introduced addressed savings responses. The 2004 Economic Report of the President (hereafter ER), Chapter 4, takes the position that capital income taxes fall, eventually, on labor, because capital income taxes reduce saving, reduce the capital stock, and cause wage income to fall. (While there is a mention of open economy issues, it is clear that the argument rests primarily on savings effects). Their argument appeals to both theory (citing the Ramsey model in particular) and to some empirical evidence, both of which are discussed in this section. See Council of Economic Advisers, *Economic Report of the President*, February 2004, pp. 110-116, at http://www.gpo.gov/fdsys/pkg/ERP-2004/pdf/ERP-2004.pdf. The February 2007 ER, Chapter 3, simply asserts this view without reference to theory or evidence. See Council of Economic Advisers, *Economic Report of the President*, February 2007, p. 82, at http://www.gpo.gov/fdsys/pkg/ERP-2007/pdf/ERP-2007.pdf.

[6] There are also growth models where growth rates are dependent on the size of the economy or certain institutional (continued...)

---

there are essentially two forms: the infinite horizon or Ramsey model, and the overlapping generations life cycle model or OLG model. (The infinite horizon model is actually a special case of the OLG model.)

These intertemporal models are commonly used in academic journals. Indeed, in macroeconomics there is increasingly a disconnect between the models used by forecasters (both private and in the government) and those used in the academic literature. Most forecasters use the basic model of sticky prices or wages where fiscal and monetary policy can affect output to address business cycles, with their models gradually developing into Solow models in the longer term. Certainly, no government or private sector forecaster uses a Ramsey or OLG model to predict economic variables.

There has also been a reaction among academic economists to these intertemporal models, which assume an enormous amount of sophistication and planning on the part of consumers, and models of "bounded rationality" have also developed, where individuals are often assumed to follow rules of thumb. These rules of thumb often lead back to the Solow model or even to a model where savings falls when the rate of return rises.

Ramsey (Infinite Horizon) Model

Because of its infinite horizon, the long run supply of savings is perfectly elastic in this model, which leads to a lot of response to a change in tax rate on capital income. The after tax rate of return must always return to its original value and the Ramsey model (when used to model the actual equilibrium in the economy rather than the social planner problem for which it was originally devised)[7] effectively depicts the economy as composed of a series of identical infinitely lived individuals who optimize over time. With a sufficiently high intertemporal substitution elasticity or IES (which measures the percentage change in the ratio of consumption in two time periods divided by the percentage change in their relative prices)[8] these effects can occur very quickly, although with more modest ones that are consistent with empirical evidence, they take place more slowly.[9]

(...continued)

features and some allow technological advance to be determined by choices within the economy (such as investment in research and development, investment in human capital, and investment in public infrastructure).

[7] Ramsey's 1928 article clearly begins by addressing the issue of the optimal amount of saving for a social planner of an economy or an economy truly composed of a single infinitely lived individual rather than describing an actual equilibrium; in fact the article contains considerable discussion of some of the problems in the model including finite lives and heterogeneous preferences. See F. P. Ramsey, "A Mathematical Theory of Savings," *The Economic Journal*, vol. 38 (December 1928), pp. 542-559. The model is also referred to as the Ramsey-Cass-Koopmans model, because of later developments in modeling, but both of these authors also referred (Cass quite explicitly) to the model as a social planner's problem rather than a description of behavior. See David Cass, "Optimum Growth in an Aggregative Model of Capital Accumulation," *The Review of Economic Studies*, vol. 32, July 1965, pp. 233-240 and Tjalling C. Koopmans, *On the Concept of Economic Growth*, Cowles Foundation Paper 238, 1965.

[8] The relative price of consumption t years into the future is $1/(1+r)t$, where r is the rate of return after tax.

[9] The 2004 ER also provides some simulations of the time path of adjustment, indicating that after five years, a quarter of the burden will fall on workers, while over ten years 40% will fall on workers. This speed of adjustment depends, among other things, on the inter-temporal elasticity of substitution (IES), which is set at one: the smaller the IES the more slowly adjustment takes place. Most empirical estimates of the IES are well below one. If a more typical value of 0.25 is chosen rather than one, the adjustment would be about half as large in the first five years (i.e., about 12 or 13% falling on wages) and about two-thirds as much after 10 years (i.e., about a quarter rather than 40%). See CRS Report RL31949, *Issues in Dynamic Revenue Estimating*, by Jane G. Gravelle, which has a review of the literature suggesting (continued...)

Life-Cycle Model

The Ramsey model is not the only way to model the effects of the capital income tax through a formal model of individual rational choice, although it is typically taught in most macroeconomics classes and is popular because of its mathematical simplicity. A more general form of inter-temporal model is the life-cycle model, where rather than depicting individuals as having a single infinite life, individuals have a finite life and new generations are born while others die. The life-cycle model has the same outcome as the Ramsey model if bequests are motivated by interdependent utility functions, but if they occur by accident, are part of a trading situation between children and parents, or because of direct utility from the gift itself ("joy of giving" motivation), the outcome will be quite different.[10]

In the life cycle model, savings may rise or fall, due to standard income and substitution effects. The life cycle model may indicate capital income taxes reduce savings or increase savings. The magnitude and direction of outcomes depend on many factors: how substitutable consumption is over time, whether individuals take into account the effects of behavioral response on future returns, why bequests occur and how they change or do not change with a change in the interest rate, the amount of savings that is for precautionary purposes rather than for retirement, the expected period of retirement relative to the working period, and the pattern of wage growth over the career, and the use of the revenues. If a tax on capital is imposed to finance spending (and that spending does not directly affect consumption behavior) then it is likely to be projected to reduce saving, but in models with a fixed bequest target that is significant, a low substitution elasticity, a lot of precautionary saving, and a long retirement period, it is perfectly possible for savings to fall. And a capital income tax cut, even were it to increase savings, would not do so to the degree arising in the Ramsey model, so that the burden would still fall partially on capital.[11] If the tax increase is used to reduce other taxes, the effects depend on the type; however, in the current U.S. federal system where the other major tax base is wages, such a tax substitution would easily increase the capital stock, even if the model did not have bequests. An increase used to reduce consumption taxes would, however tend to product a reduction in savings.[12] Raising capital income taxes and using them to reduce the deficit would almost certainly expand the capital stock (although the deficit could not grow without limit and the model cannot be solved for the steady state unless the deficit was eventually offset).

(...continued)

elasticities below 0.5; see also the review and discussion in B. Douglas Bernheim, "Taxation and Saving," originally NBER Working Paper 7061, March 1999, also published in *Handbook of Public Economics*, vol. 3 (New York: Elseiver, 2002). Also, see Eric Engen, Jane Gravelle, and Kent Smetters, "Dynamic Tax Models: Why They Do the Things They Do," *National Tax Journal*, vol. 50, September 1997, pp. 657-683, table 5, which traces the sensitivity of adjustment with respect to the intertemporal substitution elasticity.

[10] The discussion in the ER acknowledges the life cycle model when it says: "If, instead, consumers plan for their own lifetimes, savings is less responsive to changes in its after-tax rate of return and less of the capital income tax burden is shifted to workers."

[11] See also B. Douglas Bernheim, Taxation and Saving, *op. cit.* for a theoretical discussion of the factors driving elasticities in the life cycle model.

[12] See the different outcomes in Alan Auerbach and Laurence J. Kotlikoff, *Dynamic Fiscal Policy* (Cambridge: Cambridge University Press, 1987); in Jane G. Gravelle, "Income, Consumption, and Wage Taxation in a Life Cycle Model: Separating Efficiency from Redistribution," *American Economic Review*, vol. 4, September 1991, pp. 985-995; and in Eric Engen, Jane Gravelle, and Kent Smetters, "Dynamic Tax Models: Why They Do the Things They Do," *National Tax Journal*, vol. 50, September 1997, pp. 657-683.

If an increase in capital income taxes leads to decreased consumption then, rather than workers bearing part of the burden, they actually benefit, and capital income bears more than 100% of the burden.

One of the important implications of the life cycle model is that the outcome is not only sensitive to the model results, but it is also sensitive to the disposition of revenues, resulting in dramatically different outcomes depending on how revenues are used. (**Appendix A** contains a detailed discussion of why this is the case).

Comparison of Life Cycle and Ramsey Models

The life cycle model is superior to the infinite horizon model in some important respects for tax analysis (and public finance economists using intertemporal models tend to gravitate to life cycle models).[13] For example, the Ramsey model does not permit heterogeneity in preferences, unless some individuals are driven to a subsistence level, or, if borrowing against future labor income is not permitted, spend only labor income. The Ramsey model also does not work when there are differential tax rates, unless one group (a country, a state, or an income class) accumulates all of the capital. Thus, it is incompatible with differential taxes across countries, differences in state level taxes, and graduated tax rates. These problems do not exist with the life cycle model. The requirement that individuals exhibit no heterogeneity is a powerful restriction on the model. The theory also implies that with mixed bequest motives, families with bequest motives governed by interdependent utility functions will ultimately own all of the capital stock, although the steady state in the model will take much longer to reach (very long if the fraction of individuals with this type of bequest motive is small). But to reach the Ramsey solution also requires that these families have a continual unbroken dynastic link across descendants that preserves preferences and always reproduce (either asexually or by intermarrying only with other dynastic families), another strong assumption.

"Bounded Rationality"

Both models, however, present some significant other problems from a theoretical standpoint. Perhaps the most important of these is the assumption that consumers are able to engage in a process of choosing savings and consumption (and labor supply in some models) based on optimizing consumption (and leisure) over a period of 55 years or so, or even an infinite period, responding all the while to changes in current and projected wage rates, taxes, and rates of return. Since solving current models requires facility with calculus, at least the knowledge of economic modeling possessed by graduate students, and in some cases the ability to program a large scale numerical model on a computer, as well as an extensive knowledge of economic conditions, such an assumption seems difficult to defend.

Bernheim discusses a different type of model of behavior based on "bounded rationality" which acknowledges that individuals have trouble dealing with complex problems, even those much less

---

[13] The Joint Committee on Taxation chose a life cycle model for its inter-temporal model for its dynamic scoring study. (The JCT also used a reduced-form macroeconomics model). In addition, at the initial JCT symposium held in 1996, three of the four inter-temporal models were life cycle rather than infinite horizon models. See Joint Committee on Taxation, *Tax Modeling Project and 1997 Tax Symposium Papers*, November 20, 1997. The JCT also considered five reduced-form macroeconomic models. Ramsey models seem more popular among macroeconomists who are not largely dealing with tax simulations.

complex than those presented by life cycle or Ramsey models.[14] If so, those models cannot be used to assess behavior.

The response to this criticism is that individuals need only behave as if they are optimizing (much in the way that experienced poker players may behave as if they are basing their bets on the knowledge of odds even if they cannot state those odds). Bernheim describes three conditions that might permit such behavior: if individuals have a chance to repeat the behavior frequently and observe the outcome, if they can observe others' choices and outcomes easily, or if they can obtain and evaluate expert advice. The first two options do not exist for life cycle savings, which occurs only one time and without a chance to examine outcomes and behaviors of one's own contemporaries.

Financial advice is not always easy to evaluate—but more importantly, it is generally not consistent with the prescriptions of intertemporal models. Financial planners do not provide advice along the lines of the life-cycle or Ramsey models. They may recommend a rule of thumb, such as saving a percentage of income (consistent with no interest elasticity) or accumulating an appropriate annuity (which is a form of target savings which results in a rise in savings when taxes go up). A fixed saving rate is consistent with another common textbook growth model, the Solow model. It is easy to find evidence of this type of advice. For example, the National Retirement Planning Coalition posts calculators on the Internet to determine how much money you need to save to accumulate a certain recommended amount. This is a target savings approach: if the rate of return goes up you will need to save less to accumulate the target amount. Or consider these statements reported in a newspaper: "Many economists say average workers should be investing 10 to 15 percent of their pay. Other economists say no less than 25 percent";[15] and "They are nowhere near the $1 million in savings one is supposed to have for retirement." This advice proposes a fixed saving rate in the first case and a target savings approach in the second.

Special Issues with the Estate and Gift Tax

Most of the intertemporal models studied have focused on taxes on the return to capital such as individual income taxes and state and local taxes. Estate and gift taxes have unique issues: the motive can strongly determine the effect; the tax affects not only the donor but the recipient; and the estate tax is very concentrated among high-income donors.

Suppose that individuals leave bequests because they have saved money as a means of insuring against living too long or having bad health. In that case, the estate tax is irrelevant to their behavior because they will never have to face the tax. However, the estate tax may affect the savings behavior of their heirs—by reducing the value of the net bequest there is an income effect which induces more savings (or possibly more labor supply).[16] If donors receive some pleasure from giving a bequest (so that we think of a bequest as a form of individual consumption) the donor faces competing income and substitution effects that have a uncertain outcome but the

---

[14] B. Douglas Bernheim, "Taxation and Saving," *op. cit.*

[15] Betty Nooker, "Chill Descends as Boomers Rethink Retirement Plans," *Richmond Times Dispatch*, February 16, 2004.

[16] The notion that leaving descendants large bequests will cause them to be less productive citizens is referred to as the Carnegie conjecture, and it was the reason that Andrew Carnegie left most of his wealth to charity.

---

recipient has an income effect so that the tax encourages private saving. There are also exchange and altruistic models which have uncertain results.[17]

Empirical Evidence

Most empirical evidence seems to point to little savings response. The savings rate has been relatively constant during most of the post war period and attempts to formally estimate the savings response, while problematic, have found small effects of varying sign.[18] Statistical estimates of the substitution of consumption and leisure over time have suggested small effects as well.[19] These latter estimates do not directly determine the savings effects, since the effects depend on the interaction of these estimates with other model features. However, low intertemporal substitution elasticities make it hard for realistic life cycle models to produce large or even negative savings effects from capital income taxes. There is little direct evidence of the effect of estate taxes on wealth accumulation,[20] although the savings evidence in general should be informative about the estate tax as well as other capital income taxes.

As noted earlier, the 2004 Economic Report of the President (ER) has argued for the shifting of the tax to labor based largely on economic theory (and specifically referencing the Ramsey model). There is one paragraph, however, which addresses empirical evidence: "Empirical work provides some evidence that capital income taxes are shifted to some extent: studies find that the before tax return to capital is higher when the tax rate on capital income is higher. However, the picture is not entirely clear, because other factors may cause tax rates and before tax rates of return to move together." These statements were based on several papers by Casey Mulligan. The primary reference is Casey B. Mulligan, *Capital Tax Incidence: First Impressions from the Time Series*, NBER Working Paper 9374, December 2002. Secondary references were Casey B. Mulligan, *What Do Aggregate Consumption Euler Equations Say About the Capital Income Tax Burden?*, NBER Working Paper 10262, February 2004 and Casey B. Mulligan, *Capital Tax Incidence: Fisherian Impressions from the Time Series*, NBER Working Paper 9916, August 2003.

Since these papers are somewhat complicated, a careful examination of them is contained in **Appendix B**. That analysis suggests that, contrary to supporting the view that capital income taxes are shifted to labor income, the papers' evidence suggests the opposite. This assessment is based on the observation of a relatively constant estimated pre-tax return, despite significant variations in the tax rate over the twentieth century.

---

[17] See William G. Gale and Maria G. Perozek, "Do Estate Taxes Reduce Saving?" in William G. Gale, James R. Hines, Jr., and Joel Slemrod, eds., *Rethinking Estate and Gift Taxation* (Washington, DC: Brookings Institution, 2001) for a more detailed discussion.

[18] See Engen, Gravelle, and Smetters, "Dynamic Tax Models: Why They Do the Things They Do." *op. cit.*

[19] For a summary of these estimates, see CRS Report RL31949, *Issues in Dynamic Revenue Estimating*, by Jane G. Gravelle.

[20] One study found some evidence that estates are smaller as tax rates rise, but it is difficult to determine how much of that is from savings effects and how much is due to estate planning and avoidance. See Wojciech Kopczuk and Joel Slemrod, "The Impact of the Estate Tax on Wealth Accumulation," in Gale, Hines and Slemrod, *Rethinking Estate and Gift Taxation.*

Concluding Comments

This analysis suggests that the major support for the shifting of capital income tax burdens to labor income (and therefore shifting from higher- to lower-income individuals) rests in theoretical models that, while popular with many economists for their mathematical elegance, have not been empirically tested and are not consistent with most empirical evidence on saving. If a formal intertemporal model that is more realistic is used, the analysis of incidence cannot be made until the accompanying policies involving disposition of the revenues are made. For those who doubt that most individuals possess the sophistication and ability to plan (whether over a finite lifetime or an infinite family dynasty), the rule of thumb approaches that involve targeting or fixed savings rates seem consistent with bounded rationality models and suggest that capital income taxes are more likely to have little effect or increase savings. The view that there is little effect on savings seems supported by some empirical evidence.

Appendix A. The Ambiguity of Results in a Life Cycle Model

To understand the basic issues, including the uncertainty, surrounding the effect of cutting taxes on capital income using an inter-temporal model, consider a simple model where individuals live for two periods. Although more realistic multiperiod models are normally used to study tax issues, this model can provide important insights into what drives the results.

In a two period model the individual lifetime budget constraint is:

(1) $C_1 + C_2 / (1 + r(1 - t)) = WL_1 + WL_2 / (1 + r - r(1 - t))$

where C_1 and C_2 are consumption in periods one and periods two, r is the rate of return, t is the tax rate, W is the wage rate, and L_1 and L_2 are labor hours in each period. A typical utility function will result in a relationship between C_2 and C_1 as the following:

(2) $C_2 / C_1 = (B(1 + r(1 - t)))^s$

where B is the relative valuation placed on the second period consumption (B normally less than 1), indicating that future consumption is discounted in value relative to present consumption, r is the rate of return, and s is the substitution elasticity between consumption in the two periods with respect to the relative price (the price of consumption in period one is one and the price in period two is $1/(1+r(1-t))$. Also assume that L_2 and L_1 are fixed, with L_2/L_1 equal to some constant, a. If a is one, you work the same amount in both periods, and if a equals zero you are fully retired in the second period. By substituting (2) into (1) and using a you obtain the relationship between consumption and income:

(3) $C_1 (1 + B^s (1 + r(1 - t))^{(s-1)}) = WL_1 (1 + a / (1 + r(1 - t)))$

The first thing to notice about this relationship is that if a equals zero so there are no earnings in the second period, and s equals one, consumption and therefore savings is not affected by the rate of return. The effect of r on the left hand is the normal income and substitution effect of a price change (in this case, the price is $1/(1+r(1-t))$): if the rate of return goes up you may wish to consume more in the second period, but the higher return means that it is also possible to consume more in both the first and second period. The substitution effect, s, causes savings to rise and the income effect causes savings to fall. On the right hand side there is a direct income effect on W, which is called the human wealth effect. An increase in r causes the present value of earnings to fall and that effect in isolation causes consumption to fall and savings to rise when the rate of return falls. It is the relative size of these different effects that determines whether savings rises or falls with a rise in the interest rate.

If you derive the savings rate, which is $(WL_1-C_1)/WL_1$ and differentiate with respect to t and evaluate at $t = 0$ to get the change in the savings rate, that change is positive for a tax cut as long as:

(4) $s > \dfrac{1 - a(C_1/C_2)}{(1 + a/(1+r))}$

One can think of a as a parameter measuring the time horizon of earnings relative to consumption. If a equals zero, s must be greater than 1. With income in the second period, s less than one can still cause a decline in savings depending on the value of a and the other parameters. Since most empirical evidence suggests that intertemporal elasticities a quite small, there is empirical ambiguity for models where significant retirement is assumed in the second period.

The same forces that act in this two period model also act in a multi-period model that more realistically reflects actual life cycles (although the effects are much more complicated). In these models as well, the effect on savings depends on the magnitude of the intertemporal substitution elasticity and the time horizon of earnings as compared to the time horizon of consumption. This latter effect means that the period of retirement relative to the period of consumption will affect the results, that the path of wages over a lifetime will matter, and also that bequests can alter the effects because they can alter the horizons of income and consumption.

We will return to these issues after discussing a third extremely important consideration, which is how the revenues from a capital income tax increase are used (or how the loss is made up for a decrease).

Consider the following scenarios:

(1) Tax cuts on capital income reduce government spending (presumed to be spent on consumption goods) which does not affect the individual's private choices.

(3) Tax cuts on capital income reduce transfers, which may occur in the first period as well as the second period.

(4) Tax cuts on capital income are offset by tax increases on wage income.

(5) Tax cuts on capital income are made up by imposing a consumption tax.

(6) Tax cuts on capital income add to the deficit.

In each of these different scenarios a different outcome appears. Offsetting tax changes with government expenditures invokes the income and substitution effects shown above and thus a tax cut can either raise or lower savings rates.

The effect of transfers depends on whose transfers are changed. They can be changed for the old, the young, or both. To consider the two extremes, suppose a tax cut reduces transfers by the same amount for the old. In the simple two period model, the individual loses in transfers exactly what he gained in the tax cut, so that the income effects are removed. A tax cut would unambiguously increase savings for any positive intertemporal substitution elasticity.

Suppose instead that the transfer occurred in the first period. In this case, it is even less likely that a tax cut would increase savings than in the government spending case. The normal income and substitution effects that arise from increases in the rate of return would remain. But income of the young would fall because of the negative transfer and that decline in income would reduce both consumption and savings (in proportions that reflect preferences and income). Essentially this assumption produces a negative effect on the right hand side of the budget constraint much the same as a human wealth effect.

In practice, lump sum transfers of this nature are unlikely to occur. But the general nature of the transfers is associated with certain types of tax substitutions. For example, if a cut in capital income taxes is financed by a higher tax on wages, that additional tax burden is concentrated more on the young. A consumption tax places more of the burden on the old.

If the tax cut is financed by a deficit, then it is much more likely that the capital stock will fall because the effect of private savings is ambiguous but public savings will fall as a result of government borrowing. Note that a tax cut financed with a deficit can only be considered as a shorter or intermediate term effect in a model with myopic behavior (individuals believe that current wages and pre-tax returns will be fixed). For a long run steady state some resolution of that deficit must be determined.

There are many aspects of a life cycle model that will affect the direction and magnitude of the effect on savings. The following is a partial list of model features and assumptions that will contribute to the likelihood that the model would predict a savings decrease with a cut in capital income taxes:

(1) Lower intertemporal substitution elasticities.

(2) Tax cut offset by higher wage taxes, or by a deficit eventually resolved by restoring higher tax rates.

(3) Including bequests, which tend to lengthen the time horizon between consumption and earnings (as long as bequests do not arise from interdependent utility functions which leads to the Ramsey model discussed in the text). The effect of bequests is particularly likely to push the results towards less savings when they tend to be fixed targets, as might be the case when money is accumulated because of uninsurable uncertainties such as longevity and health in old age.

(4) Incorporating risk which cannot be eliminated by market mechanisms. This could be risk in wage earnings, risk in expectancy, health, rate of return or any number of uncertainties. Risk not only leads to the accumulation of precautionary savings that is not very sensitive to the rate of return (and indeed may be more affected by income effects from the interest rate) but also leads to accumulation of bequests as a form of self-insurance which also tend to be insensitive, as noted above.

(5) Longer retirement period relative to working period, which expands the time horizon of consumption relative to earnings.

(6) Slower productivity growth (which slows the growth of expected wages); and in general a wage profile with declining wages in later years.

(7) Assumption of a minimum subsistence amount of consumption in each period, which limits substitutability in consumption (referred to as the Stone-Geary utility function).

There are many other uncertainties associated with life cycle models, some of these quite technical in nature. It is difficult, for example, to calibrate a life cycle model to match all of the features of the economy without bequests unless intertemporal elasticities are set relatively high (even if empirical evidence suggests they are low),[21] growth rates are set artificially low, the time

---

[21] For a survey of evidence on the intertemporal substitution elasticity, see CRS Report RL31949, *Issues in Dynamic* (continued...)

preference rate is negative, or the capital-output ratio is not realistic. All of those compromises affect outcomes in important ways, and it might be argued that any life cycle model that does not include bequests is deeply flawed as a model of savings behavior even if other concerns were not present. In a model that did include bequests, it was quite common to find that a shift to wage tax decreased the capital stock.[22]

(...continued)

Revenue Estimating, by Jane G. Gravelle.

[22] See Jane G. Gravelle, "Income, Consumption, and Wage Taxation in a Life-Cycle Model: Separating Efficiency from Redistribution," American Economic Review, vol. 81, September 1991, pp. 985-995.

Appendix B. Evaluation of the Empirical Evidence Referenced in the 2004 Economic Report of the President (ER)

Turning to the primary reference[23] (the other papers are in the same vein), the empirical evidence that is referred to in the ER report and that is the main subject of Mulligan's paper, addresses a different shifting issue altogether, namely whether firms try to mark up prices in the short run to immediately shift the burden to consumer prices. This type of short-run shifting is generally questioned by economists, because it requires firms to make irrational short run decisions. If firms are maximizing their profits before tax, then any change in prices leads to a smaller profit and adds a loss in pre-tax profit to the tax burden itself. Also if firms are in a competitive environment, it is difficult to be successful in raising prices because sales would decline significantly.

Despite these reservations, a study in the 1960s argued that there was evidence for short run shifting of the corporate tax,[24] although most economists studying the issue concluded that the effects were due to not controlling for other factors, particularly cyclical factors.

The Mulligan paper actually carried out two different empirical estimates. The following is a summary and commentary on these findings.

Regressing Pre-Tax Profits Against Tax Rates

The paper begins with calculations of the pre-tax return to capital and the overall average tax rate on capital taken from the National Income and Product Accounts. Noting that the after tax return is r(1-t), where r is the pretax return and t is the tax rate, he regresses the log of r against the log of (1-t). A coefficient of minus one would indicate that the entire tax is shifted (i.e., the after tax return remains constant), and a coefficient of zero would indicate no shifting. He presents a scatter diagram of the average of these values for five year intervals, and his regression initially yields a coefficient of -0.27 (which would suggest about 27% is shifted). However, a visual examination of the scatter diagram contained in Mulligan's paper makes it clear that the regression coefficient is caused by two outlying periods reflecting World War II (1941-1945) and the Great Depression (1931-1935), and Mulligan suggests those periods be excluded. Once those periods are excluded, the regression line would appear to have an approximate zero coefficient—that is, although the tax rate changes substantially, there is little variation in the pre-tax returns. In particular, the rate of return early in the century is no different than later returns, even though tax rates were zero at that point.

Rather than running the regression on this set of data, which would almost certainly produce an insignificant coefficient around zero, the author decides to exclude all pre-World War II data. His reason for doing so is that the data are not as reliable. However, this exclusion also eliminates much of the variability of the tax rate data. The new regression line has a coefficient of -0.51

---

[23] Casey B. Mulligan, *Capital Tax Incidence: First Impressions from the Time Series*, NBER, Working Paper 9374, December 2002.

[24] Marian Krzyzaniak and Richard A. Musgrave, *The Shifting of the Corporate Income Tax* (Baltimore, MD, 1963).

suggesting half of the tax is shifted. However, it is apparent, again, from looking at the scatter diagram, that cyclical effects are still at work—for example, the 1981-85 period which covers a serious recession is characterized by low pre-tax returns and low tax rates, just as the case of the Great Depression. When Mulligan controls for forecasted unemployment, the relationship disappears with the coefficient not statistically different from zero (and actually positive).

These data, therefore, tend to indicate that there is no short-run shifting—that is, pretax returns are not high when tax rates are high. The simple data also would not appear to present much of a case for long run shifting either, since the pre-tax return did not change over long periods of time. That is, tax rates went from zero and very low rates to fairly high rates, over a period covering many years, but there seemed to be little change in pre-tax returns. Mulligan does not use this data to address the long run issue (and there are many other factors that could have an effect). So how is it that Mulligan concludes that there is evidence of long run shifting? (His abstract states: The empirical findings are consistent with significant capital tax shifting in the long run, little shifting in the short run, and clearly rule out over-shifting.)

Euler Equation Regressions

This conclusion apparently arises from the second part of the paper (and actually from references to other work) which turns to a different estimating strategy. Instead of using pre-tax returns and tax rates, the analysis looks at consumption growth, using the consumption Euler equation from the first order conditions of an intertemporal model (using expectations). This first order condition is:

(1) $\ln E(C_t/(C_{t-1}) = E (s (r(1-t) -p))$

which says that the expected growth rate in consumption (C) is determined by the expected after tax rate of return, and s is the Intertemporal Elasticity of Substitution (IES).

It is not possible using this approach to differentiate between the effect of the IES on growth and the short run shifting of the tax. That is, the growth rate of consumption might be unaffected by the tax rate because the IES is close to zero or because a change in r offsets a change in t (short run shifting). Mulligan uses estimates from another paper to set the IES to 1 by regressing consumption growth against after-tax income—an estimate that itself comes from a paper using similar data and that might be questioned.[25] In this case [because he regresses consumption growth against the log of (1-t)] a coefficient of zero implies there is short run shifting and a coefficient of 0.08 (equal to the after tax return) suggests that there is no shifting.

---

[25] This paper essentially uses the same data to estimate the IES, but actually regresses it against the after-tax return. See Casey B. Mulligan, *Capital Interest, and Aggregate Inter-temporal Substitution*, National Bureau of Economic Research, Working Paper 9373, December 2002. The main innovation of this paper is that the author uses constructed tax rates for the entire capital stock, rather than financial returns, since he argues that a more complete portfolio provides a better measure of after-tax returns. (Of course such a portfolio could also be measured as a mix of after tax financial assets with the exception of owner-occupied housing and noncorporate equity, thereby avoiding at least some potential measurement error). The scatter diagram presented in that paper (covering 1930-1997) also shows the depression and war years to be outliers (and thus results in a much higher IES when those years are included). The elasticities around one come from a 1947-1997 simulation. The scatter diagram also seems to suggest that cyclical effects are at work here as well, but no adjustment for made for them. As noted earlier, most of the body of empirical work, including those using micro-economic panel data, suggests a low IES.

The results are mixed and since he is using the same data set for estimating both the IES and short run shifting, it is not clear what the findings are. And although claims are made about long run shifting, it seems difficult to reconcile these results with the data from the first part of his study, which seems to show that pre-tax returns do not change very much over long periods of time. Mulligan concludes that "the empirical findings are consistent with significant capital tax shifting in the long run, little shifting in the short run, and clearly rule out over-shifting." It appears that his conclusions about the long term arise from the fact that tax rates have varied but consumption growth has not. If one assumes a significant IES and no other disturbances (arising, for example, from demographic or technological changes) then one could interpret the stability of consumption growth over periods far apart as evidence that the tax was shifted over the long run. However, the data in his scatter diagram that directly relate pretax return to net of tax share, seem to contradict that view, indicating that, when leaving out the depression and war years and controlling for unemployment, there is no effect of taxes on the pre-tax return, a view consistent with no effect on saving.

Direct evidence of long run effects of tax changes on savings is difficult to find given the limitations of data. A number of studies have tried to relate the savings rate to the after tax rate of return; those studies have mostly found small effects that vary in sign—that is small increases or small decreases, but none very significant.[26] These results are not consistent with significant long term shifting, but there are problems with these approaches. In particular, they came under criticism because of arguments that policy changes and expectations might not be constant over time (the Lucas critique). Some of these same criticisms could be applied to comparing pre-tax rates of return over time.

The other approach, a consumption Euler approach, as discussed in the Mulligan paper is also vulnerable to many criticisms.[27] Certainly one of them is the possibility that tax rate changes are unanticipated shocks and an uncertainty about the purpose of the tax change. Suppose we presume that the infinite horizon model holds and that there is no short run shifting. An unanticipated fall in the marginal tax rate on capital income that is expected to be permanent (let us in this example hold total taxes constant) causes current consumption to fall in a way that is divorced from the Euler equation, and is set to move the economy to a new growth path. Consumption would fall all at once. Then consumption growth would be higher because the rate of return is higher. But this higher growth would gradually slow as the rate of return adjusted until a new steady state was reached. Thus the theoretical model that lies behind the estimates using the Euler equations, suggests that if the IES is actually large (i.e., one) then consumption growth must be a function of profits as well as tax. If the rate of return is to be fixed or virtually fixed, the implication is that the IES is virtually zero—which means that either the Ramsey model adjusts so slowly that it takes centuries to reach a new equilibrium, or that the Ramsey model is not the right model. Moreover, the presumption of an IES of one in this section is not consistent with the findings in the section comparing pre-tax returns with tax rates. That data seemed to show a relatively constant pre-tax return, an outcome consistent with a very low IES or a model where taxes do not affect savings rates, such as the model of bounded rationality where individuals save a target fraction of income or target an annuity.

---

[26] See Engen, Gravelle, and Smetters, "Dynamic Tax Models: Why They Do the Things They Do," *op.cit.*

[27] See B. Douglas Bernheim, "Taxation and Saving," *op. cit.* for a discussion of the problems of estimating elasticities, particularly with aggregated consumption.

Summing Up

A number of other issues might be raised about the Mulligan paper, including the fact that aggregate consumption growth is affected by technology and population growth, as well as many other institutional factors. Moreover, the author does not actually measure the marginal tax rates that should drive the savings response (he uses average rates). Taxes also include the property tax rate, which is problematic on a number of grounds (including the possibility that these tax rates are capitalized or that individuals choose to live in places where property tax rates are set so as to provide a desirable bundle of local government services).

Overall, however, the most straightforward conclusion from this empirical paper is that the pre-tax return has been remarkably stable over a long period of time and in the post-war period when controlled for cycles. This evidence seems to suggest not only that taxes are not shifted in the short run, but also that they do not induce the savings behavior that results in a shift in the long run. If so, the tax burden would fall on owners of capital, not on labor

Author Contact Information

Jane G. Gravelle
Senior Specialist in Economic Policy
jgravelle@crs.loc.gov, 7-7829

Sean Lowry
Analyst in Public Finance
slowry@crs.loc.gov, 7-9154